Scraps of Love

Poetry from the Darkest Night

1997-2010

Shann Tajiah

Ithirial Rising Press

Texas

Additional Publications

The Balance of Life
1997 Honorable Mention Award, Iliad Press (Cader Publishing)
W.S.G. Newsline, September 1997
H.E.I.R. Newsline, October 1997
1998 President's Award for Literary Excellence, Iliad Press (Cader Publishing)
Bitter Rain, Black Hole, Galaxy of You, Mysti, Paper Angel Wings, Skeleton in the Closet, Thunderbolt of Desire, Tragic Blooming
Literatus World Review Webzine, McGraw Publishing, January 2001
The Red Pill
Highland Poetry Quarterly, Vol. 1, Issue 1, April 2001

Author photograph © TjaEssence Photography & Arts, used with permission
Cover Design by Shann Tajiah – Typography by Hineni Asah
Cover photo image used under license from shutterstock.com

ISBN-10: 978-1-962898-00-3

First Edition: September 2018
Second Edition eBook: August 2022
Second Edition Paperback: February 2024
Some poems have been removed, moved to a different location for readability, or edited in the Second Edition

For more information please contact:
ithirialrisingpress@gmail.com

For all survivors,
you are not alone.

Charlene,
thank you for teaching us
that we can live out loud.

Table of Contents

Author's Note

My little lamb is sad today,
he doesn't even want to play!
If I give him some hay,
"baa baa" he will say!
- My Little Lamb, Age 8

It was a school project in 1992 when I wrote my first poem. At that time, I didn't even know what a poem was, and I was horribly frightened at the thought of having to create one. In the end I was proud of myself but had vowed to never write a poem ever again. I had no idea that poetry would eventually become my voice.

I come from a broken home, born into a family that harbored many secrets, and within that silence, more abuse festered. I was raised with a skewed view of what love was, what boundaries were, and who owned my physical body, my soul, and my future. Daily I was quietly fracturing as I continued to endure not only neglect, but sexual, physical, verbal, and spiritual abuse.

My first brush with poetry was long forgotten until 1997. I met a young man online who seemed to mirror my darkness with his own writings. During my short friendship with H.C., I began to find my own poetic voice.

Through my poetry I began to make new friends who were walking painful paths like I was. Andrew, Jodee, Kaosha, Sam, Lynsie, Malcolm and Heather became a huge part of my healing journey. They stand in my Hall of Heroes because they did what no one else ever had. They supported and understood my writing, and the need that drove me to paint with words.

Previous attempts to keep journals, write novels, or reach out for help were met with accusations, more violent abuse, and even death threats and attempts. Poetry became my escape – the abstract medium that could free me even as I continued to learn that there was no escape from "real life" and that my idea of what reality should be was a fantasy.

By the time I was eighteen, I had convinced myself that I was crazy. I was experiencing intense panic attacks that always lead to blackouts. I had already attempted to take my own life on four occasions and had been left to sleep it off instead of being brought to the E.R. When forced into therapy, my family unit was so skilled at hiding the truth, that therapists were unsure why we had been referred to them in the first place. It was a vicious circle.

My life felt hopeless, completely out of control. I struggled with the dissonance of believing what was happening to me was my fault and the completely opposite, intense feelings that nothing going on was right or normal. In addition, I was suddenly uncertain how to reconcile my deeply religious upbringing and legalistic family, with an Elohim that would allow me to endure abuses that violated every part of me time and time again.

I continued to turn to poetry to try and make sense of what was happening in my life. But the pressure to stop writing, and the adult corporate world of over-time, stress, and over-achieving soon led to a breakdown that left me homeless and suicidal. I was completely broken, and Yahweh showed up and really started working in my life.

Today I can say, "Where I am now, is not where I have been."

I feel so blessed to be learning how to live with freedom. Finally, I am free of the people that have hurt me, and through therapy, I am learning how to create a life on my terms. That is what publishing this collection is about.

I'm aware that the themes of some of these poems may seem juvenile to some, not "real poetry" to others, or may even be seen as revenge, but that's not why I am preserving them in this way. As I rediscovered and rescued the stacks of moldy, wet papers from my flooded storage shed this summer, the passion to see my works published was renewed. It seemed like a second chance to not only move beyond the fear of discovery and the fear of judgement, but also an opportunity to finally break the silence that I had been trained to keep. It seemed like now was the time to set my voice free and tell my story of fighting towards freedom, a step of acceptance that the past cannot be undone, but it can be left behind.

I chose to present this collection backwards and arranged the works within the years and in the order that they were created. My hope is to reflect the chaotic emotions, opinions, and thoughts that I was experiencing moment to moment as I lived the highs and lows of survival. I hope I was successful in giving you at least a taste of what it was like, and what it is still sometimes like in my wild mind.

Thank you for reading this book with compassion and for accepting the invitation to tour my inner garden world. Thank you for allowing me to take you back in time to meet a young girl, writing in the secret of darkness as she ached from her last beating, and waited for the next unwelcome visit to her bed.

- Shann Tajiah, 2018

2010

...we are running from something I don't understand...

Lies

I can't cry anymore
time, and love, and pain
have become like
snow to fire
turning hot blue flame
to naught.

This is what you do best,
bringing out the worst in me.
Where I am
becomes where I've been.
I've learned to be like you
again
and even more.

I thought I had so much,
but only held your lies.
Lies that you were greedy for.
Lies you couldn't even leave
me, to ease this empty thing
I've become.

You took everything when
you walked away.

I gave you so much
when you walked into my life.
A ghost of a child,

unable to be denied.

You stole so much
when you walked away,
a broken shadow
of what you're destined to be.

I hope you feel the weight
of my heart pressing you
on the days that I need ~~want~~
you the most.

I hope one day you feel
regret for leaving
all of you.

Sin Eater

Disgust marks me,
brands me,
reminds me
why you can never let me be.

Always breathing,
your presence shivers
down my spine.
It reminds me why
I disappear from your view.

You'll blame me,
you always have.
Let me be the Sin Eater,
for this whole clan.
I expect nothing less
and honestly
want nothing more
than your assumptions
and judgments
while I hide from your view.

It took too long
to get where I've been.
It took too long
for you to request
another round.

I'm not who I've been,
you're not who I'll be.
You're still stuck
in the quagmire with
the demons that hitchhike,
the lies that bind,
the fears that blind.

And disgust marks me,
as I yearn to be free
forever.

Here to Save Me

I stand on a pale world
of blues and pinks
and violets.
Everything seems muted here,
touch, and taste
and smell.
My gaze is captured by foggy
worlds hovering in orbit
about me.
They linger on the horizon
covered in swirls of colors.

For all the beauty of this
peaceful, demure place
we are running from something
I don't understand.

It walks like man
and talks like man
but is infected and
have become something else...
something Other.

Eyes glow
from sunken sockets.
Skin dry and stretched,

glossy like treated leather.
Weathered like mummies
but alive somehow, still.

They threaten us somehow,
in ways I do not know.
They seek to infect us
all
so the propaganda says.

I try to protect you
but are too tempted
by the sweets they offer.
You succumb
one bite of forbidden fruit
and you change before my eyes.

I run away.
But you catch me up,
and run, your transformation
complete.
In your arms I feel
no threat
just the speed
as you run so fast
only colors are visible
about us.

You speak to me,
but I cannot hear your words.
Your grip so tight,
on the edge of pain,
but I know you're protecting me.
I feel no fear.
Somehow I know
you will not change me,
your metamorphosis came to save me.

We are still running
when I awaken
from my dream pale hues
of blues, and pinks, and violets.
And I wonder who you are
when I return to Earth.

Return to Them

The darkness, so inviting.
It beckons
again.
Essence like silky chocolate
melting on the tongue
at first,
but bitter in the last
throws of passion.

I could claw my eyes away,
could strip this flesh
from my form
if that was the sacrifice needed
to endure.

But the truth is:
You can't go home
and people never change.

Inspired by Dreams and Visions

I

lost myself among the
overgrown maze that ripped and
violated my covering, tearing at my skin
excavating the blood that flows beneath my flesh

Yellow light hints at dawn, but it never breaks
over the horizon, it just lingers
understanding all of my desires

Sweet dreams called to me, so I
took your passive hand in mine
in faith I
let myself fall into you, and
lurid tones of warning faded until unheard.

2007

...How can you ignore the wounds
dripping crimson when

you're next...

Bitter Wines

I can't sleep tonight.
The abstract,
time subjective,
dreams
dependent on choices,
nightmares
(maybe your tears)
so many angry accusations.

Hearts marinated in lies,
salted and raw,
twined up with bitter herbs,
you say we can save each other.

I told lies too.
Believed your lies more.
I painted my soul with them,
held them close.
Held them in deep silence,
disguised them with strength and patience.
Stubborn ~~survivors~~ victims,
afraid of losing humanity
while eating each other alive.
The bitter wine of
Love
Hate
Despair

pours over
through
around
a drowning, heavy death.
A secret death.
these lies still hiding our truth.

Fear is the greatest enemy.
Not our pasts.
Never our future.

Next

You defend them like they're right,
you judge me like I'm wrong,
renting lies in poverty.
Too bad for you,
I feel so sorry.

You react like they are wronged,
but their smiles have a trace of blood.
How can you ignore the wounds
dripping crimson
when you're next?

2006

...For you, I'm a million names so you can place your shame and tears on one alter...

Velvet Death

You were forbidden fruit.
So like the almond blossom
you cradled in your palm
and teased with gentleness.
While the whole world could see
what she couldn't believe,
that you held velvet death.

Briar Rose

It sounds like a fairytale.
Just another Briar Rose
pulling out her thorns.
Another wounded girl
fleeing from that cliché past.
Too bad it is me...
too bad, you can't truly see

It's real
and it burns with
acid fire
consumes all - destroying
all that is me.
All I can see
are the wounds you carved.

One Alter

FOR SHANN

I don't need you
and I find it kind of funny
that you need me.
That you want me for what I can deliver,
but only when I'm here.

It's never easy, I'm
either used or lonely.
I choose one evil or another,
but for both I'm a million names,
crazy, and unstable
just so you can place your blame and fears
on one alter

I don't pretend
to be the one I need.
I'm never out there, never what I need to be.

It is never simple.
The way you turn away
like I'm a leper.
You create a disease
for you, I'm a million names,
rejected, and regret
so you can place your shame and tears
on one alter

2005

...Cover me like mist in shadows and bare me under your love...

Loving Travels

Travel beneath my skin,
discover my soul's symphony,
and explore my heart's mystery.
Don't be my judge
instead;
cover me like
mist in shadows
beneath the winter sky.
And wrap me up in
all that is you
and bare me
under your love.

2010

...You are here,

       resting so deep...

All or Nothing

Anger, resentment and power
lull me to sleep each night,
lighting my way to tomorrow.

Organs pulse, hot and steady,
reminding consistently that it's not over. They are

never to be left behind,
over the line you dictate.
These secrets cannot be
held much longer
in the darkness. They're
nudging, trampling to be free. Needing
greatness in the light.

It's All or Nothing,
and they want All.
They want Now.

Today

Today is okay.
You're not here,
to scream in my ear.

Today I forget.
The sky is bright,
clouds far away.

You still have me,
but not held as close.
Today holds promise.
I have hope,
I can be free again.

Today I forget
the sound of
your voice.

You still have me,
but not as close.

Needy

FOR ASH, JANA, IRISH, MISTY & SHANNANIGAN

You're here
resting so deep,
so quietly
I almost fool myself
into thinking you're not real.

Your breaths match mine,
our eyes blink in tandem.
We are the same,
yet different.
We are together,
yet estranged.

We are nothing without
the other.
You even my breaths,
you calm my nerves,
you care   you love.

All I do is *need*,
but that's okay,
because you know me,   and I love you.

Silence

Quiet, quiet
silence deep
swallowing me whole
even though incomplete.

Quiet blinds
my Self, my view.
Every nightmare
true.

Not At All

You're not letting me change,
not really.
The words sound so pretty
falling from your mouth,
but you follow every praise
with negatives.

You're not letting me grow,
not at all.
My skin is pruning,
there's too much water.
I'm rotting, but you don't care.
You just want me to stay.

Suitcase

I heard your suitcase
say *goodbye*
as you walked away
without a word.

You abandon me
among the ruins,
the reminder of the
chaos you created.

You're my worst mistake.
Seeking your love
my thoughtless act.
You never cared.
Clearly,
because it was your suitcase
that said *goodbye*.

Branded

I wish it was you,
standing here branded.
I wish it was you,
breathing this
rancid air.

I wish there was
some way to pull you
into my nightmare,
so you could really see and
finally understand
this constant death.

I wish you knew what
compassion was.
I wish I could teach you what is real.

I want this dance to end,
this dizzying reel
that makes me wear
my soul on my shirt.

I want you to stop pretending,
I want to be able to love you again.
I want to have one good memory of you.
I want you to tell the truth.
Please stop destroying me.

2003

...I never loved you any more than I do now,
never hated you less...

<u>Worldly</u>

Human suppression teaches
crime and murder.
Addiction doubts the solution (truth).

The world (around)
preaches wars and desires.
Contentment, unlivable religion.

Clearer Vision

Same old story,
same old shames.
Nothing has changed,
just me.

My feelings are so much
stronger,
but I'm in control.
Come a little closer,
get a clearer view.
No more time for games,
no more belief in lies.
I'm in control.

Same old story,
same old fears.
Nothing has changed,
just the way I look at you.

Cry

Wilting on the stem that grew me,
falling to the ground that nourished me.
I'm not gone; I'm still here
among the flowers and the trees.
It's okay to miss me,
but let me fly on your memory.

It's okay to cry.

Dream that I'm the sun shining through the raindrops,
see me as the colors of the rainbow.
Vibrant in all you see
your love still complete.
It's okay to miss me,
but let me fly on your memory

It's okay to cry.

Even the clouds can't keep forming
without learning how to cry,
they're really no different from you and I.
Let the sorrow wash over you
beneath the angry sky;
remember
they're really no different from you and I.

Aurora

The colors break the heavens
with tangling nerves

Elsewhere we touch
beyond time and harm

Let Go

I should be lying on my face
covered with your shame,
but I am standing on my own
making you so wrong.
So you're the victim of it all?
I don't buy your bloody tale
whosoever does isn't mine.

The sun fell on your moon,
the stars to your ground,
everything upside down.

I don't care.
I bowed down for far too long,
drowning in despair.
You need to let go
of all your lies,
just look around,
you're standing all alone.

You tore me from the inside out,
you made me cry.

You laughed out loud as I began
to wither, to die.
I'm still the victim of your lies,
but the walls are getting thin,
I can see escape.

The sun is rising on my ocean,
the stars rising on my calling
even as it all seems upside down.

I don't care.
I've groveled and I've courted you
for nothing but despair.
I know how to let go
of all your lies,
I look inside
thanks to you
I'm not alone.

Never More, Never Less

Looking anywhere
for inspiration.
Ignoring my insides;
I'm so tired of going round
and around,
reliving our ties.

I never loved you
any more than I do now,
never hated you less.
On never-ending
reliving our every kiss.

It's saying a lot
for me to want to forget.
It explains all you are
and of the weakness in my chest.

It's never been more,
never less.
It's never gone,
but never here.
You are always with my
every motive, my every nerve.
Will I always look behind me
to see you aiming for my back?
You were never harmless,
were never harm,
but there was always cause
for fear.
Some things never change,
some people never heal.

2002

...Life is written in ink...

Pass Me By

Quietly pass me by,
whisper not the lie
that paints your lips
like crimson tears.

So you question your worth
over and over.
Don't let Sadness give birth,
there's always a sunrise.

Secretly give release
into the air
that meets your breath
like gentle wings.

Do you have to break your heart
over and over?
Don't give birth to pain,
there's always tomorrow.

Here and Now,
Now and Then
seem to blur
into Forever.
Make it stop,
take a breath.

Now and Then,
Here and Now
brought to death
on the mind
and the heart
like snow under the sun.

There's always tomorrow.

The Black Piper of the Battlefield

The stunning cold,
of finding yourself back at the beginning.

Sharp, twisted terrors
creep through me,
entwining about my bones
like jellyfish.

Quiet exhaustion
looms over me,
dragging my every step.

A quiet normalcy
that dreams of growing stronger
diminishes like smoke on the winds of Spring.
These rebirth months are overtaken by
doubts and fears.

"Quiet!"
Whisper I into the night,
yearning for a Moment's rest
even though it seems intangible.

The only thing to be touched
tasted
heard
are the voices of the past.
They're urging me to give up my sword
and surrender on my knees,
hands open and accepting the predetermined fate.

They whisper that I will be a pawn no longer,
that my secrets will lie safe inside me,
but their words ring through me,
and I cannot accept them as Truth.

"Good things will follow", they say.
I cut off my legs so I am unable to follow The Piper
like so many mice.

Your music is twisted
but so very alluring.
I quiet all that is in me
to hear you sing such deceits.
Then
I swing up my sword
crippled at your feet
Undefeated.

Last Dance

Dipping,
revolving,
feet consuming the floor.
Movement smoother than honey,
ecstasy of love in
fluid motion.

Dangerous abandon
swirls through my veins.
Your hands press me closer,
lips caress my neck.

Those who stand by watching
condense to small points,
their words of warning fade,
my universe is spun gently
on a loving axis.

Our hands entwine
just as our breaths mingle.
My palm presses against your back,
holding you tight against my heart.

Our spinning movements slow,
your grip on me becomes dispassionate.
You step back,
until only our hands and eyes link.
A hardness echoes through your gaze
before it lowers to the floor.

Your fingers loosen,
releasing me.
You carry yourself away,
leaving me standing on this abandoned floor.

I turn to tears,
vibrating with the music.

Frozen Silence

You see my dying,
caught to the knees in snow.
I watch you walk away
one with the wind.
I taste your coldness on my lips
as you leave me standing
among diamond sharp snowflakes.

Inside
I float like the crystallized water
of air, then
tumble through winter silence.

I remain,
cold, fragile of form,
frozen like no other.

Naked

The fog is lifting,
burned away by a hotter face.
Naked now,
I stand, my robes gone
like they had never flowed around me.
I am so thankful for the fullness
of the trees,
and try not to remember the
landscape of the harsher season.

Demise

The monster beneath this dress
is hidden by smooth beauty,
cool as winter rain.

You receive her black kiss
in a summer moon garden
of seduction.
The water turns to red rust
as your ecstasy rings through the night.

Consume Me

Consume me.
Take the breath from
my lungs and be my oxygen.
Consume me. Learn the beat of my heart.

Take all that is bad,
remove my discontent.
Keep me centered on you,
through pain
and joy.
I am yours
and you are mine.
To consume
and be consumed.
To be one
and not alone.

Consume me,
and make me burn with desire.

Enchanted Time

The heart never forgets,
this mind never sleeps.
Those tears stopped yesterday,
this agony becomes mute.

A time so enchanted
that it can't be erased.
I'll always remember the look of your face.

The taste of you is faded,
never to be tasted again.
But the love is held dear, and my sorrow doesn't consume.
I don't feel that you've locked me
in an empty room.

Enchanted time holds for me another,
who's taste is so intoxicating,
and his embrace will turn me to liquid fire.
The heart never forgets . . . .
but the tears stopped yesterday.

Teardrop

Dripping down my face,
this physical rain
so hot, it's burning.

Teardrop on the fire
of my contrition.
Teardrop on the ice
of your shame.
Through rivers of blood
we see.

Teardrop on the face
of the dreamer,
where beginnings and endings
are never kissed away.

Celestial Born

Born to the stars,
shimmering, or falling.
Burning for the passions
that bring brilliance
or death.

Watch the dance of shining lights
knowing
no one will say this is the
future you can grasp.
Over the hill your lover waits
for your calling.

Born for the stars,
shining and falling.
Born for your time of brilliance.

Antiquity

Silky hands run over
dusty marble.
Gentle creases absorbing the past
with reverence.

Soft eyes tearfully desire
the faded past
to grow young again, while the hands
love the age.

White Water

Here we stand,
the rapids rush between us.
Tumbling, tumbling
blue, white, green.
Rushing
to No Man's Land.

Do not try to cross,
you'll be swept away.
I cannot walk away,
and release pride held in vain.
I step into the torrent then
tumble, tumble.
Rushing
to No Man's Land.

I am tossed wildly
in the blue,
under gray-black skies.
The underwater echo
fills my ears with liquid sound
as you call my name.
I cannot stop.
I'm rushing, rushing
far from your hand.

Voices

Wipe that shade of despair from your eye,
it's time to pretend.
Keep that voice light, they're watching!

Those critical voices bounce against skull,
making them heard at any cost.
The desire for one voice
becomes almost void
as it drifts away from this insanity.

The voices scream louder,
reminding, always reminding
of a love that could have saved you.
You protest that you forgot the words,
but it's too apparent that you weren't good enough...

Or so they say.

Voices are only as intelligent as
the mind behind them,
and you know better.

Ink Lines

I'm weak and frail,
it's hardly intended.
Suppressed for so long,
has rendered my spirit faded.
Too bad I'm a hazard to
your truth.

Walking away looks so inviting,
if only the path was untouched by your dirt.
Even my skin is stained by your sin,
and running is hardly any cure
for this disease, unending.

The itch to strike my story from all,
a fantasy.
Life is written in ink.
Fragile seconds, so freely wasted,
with this breath, ten more disappear.

Loss

Once upon a time
I heard your
voice deep in my soul.

But now the voice is silent,
you don't need me anymore.
The last time you understood me
was so long ago
I can't recall.

You turn your face away,
ignoring my plea for
palm against palm,
spirit against spirit.

This path I'm forced on
will damn me for eternity,
while I watch you flourish.

Highway

Too far gone to care that
your tears are flowing
in my direction.
For far too long I've
murdered my time,
now I'll choose living.

The highway begins to sing outside my window
at 3 A.M.
The call to place my feet
against the oiled ground
creates an irksome itch.

I want only the movement of
air to carry the smell of grass and blue sky,
not of your fetid breath.

The song of the highway
calls for my journey to begin.
I follow -
the oiled path kinder to my feet
than any meadow.

Beyond Belief

My hands are finally dry now,
free of the blood-letting
(my own).
With relief I can taste
the Summer breeze
before it makes way for Fall.

Today, living dangerously
has given way to living
quietly, in harmony.
I can hear the colors now
before they meet my eyes.

In all the things there used to be,
not one brought a moment of
pleasure (sadly I contemplate).
To be in such misery,
such desolation,
is almost beyond my belief
(despite having lived it).
How can I expect you to believe?

The Lament

You cry for your slippers,
the ones you lost to use.
In the darkness your eulogy
for the leather
reaches my ears.

I speak of my heart,
the one I lost to silence.
In the darkness my pain
is drowned
by your replaceable loss.

Wasteland

An illusion of peace hovers
just against the horizon.
This red wasteland plays games with the mind,
pulling secret fantasies into Nothing
after deception falls.

Mindless ravings rush forth,
their barbs strike their marks
as I set self-disgust free.
Once more, hope was allowed,
but this red planet is unyielding
and harsh to my every need.

Time flows through me,
each moment anticipating my destruction.
I begin to bury my soul deep,
denying the land its pleasures.

And I wait to taste that last,
sweet breath.

<u>Touch</u>

I touch the stars,
I know you're here.
I can feel you burning through me.

I fly so high,
I know you're here.
I can feel you dreaming.

I know you can't be too far.

I feel your heart,
so close to mine.
Your rhythm beats through me.
I hear my name,
fall from your lips.
No sound could be sweeter.

And I know you can't be too far
out of reach.
One more breath and we can touch
(the stars).

Catalyst

The cold winds of Autumn
make the tiny hairs
on my arm
wave like tall field grasses.

My skin shivers with each brush.

I welcome the cold;
somehow it matches
all that's in me.
The need for death
to bring rest,
to bring forth life.

April 23, 2002

A quiet, solid yearning,
alights my path.
Simple silence
hails the dreamer
nestling in my breast,
she's always dreaming of cutting away.

Justice guides me
over the mountains,
leaving pain in dim memory.
Innocence gone, I calm the yearning that
is ever calling for the past.

Morning beckons and offers solace
and the Eternal Peace
my dreams only sought
in the blanket under burning stars.
So I am not yearning
or seeking new beginnings,
instead I make these endless roads my own.

Tragic Blooming

Locked in the morning silence,
within my lost land of desire.
Remembering
you walking barefoot in the lingering dew.

A blue reality bloomed with tragedy
the lilac's innocence losing time,
a delicious love ended.

Inconceivable Freedom

Buried
in the graveyard of hunger.
My body lays stiff and cold,
somehow the winds above penetrate my coffin.

This part is dead
and still it won't rest.
It refuses to go
where all self-born demons should be banished.

Instead I am the disowned.

All connections have been severed,
save the bell that stands beside the headstone.
Silver quiet peels are heard faintly down here,
swinging in the wind,
not by the string connected to my paralyzed finger.

In the graveyard of hunger,
I yearn. I wait.
I am silenced.

Angel

Upon the threshold
silken Scintillation stood.

Countless gazed, wide-eyed,
desiring the facets of immortality.

In wonder,
I drank of their mortal nectar.
Then fled the flesh,
wingless
and bereft of love.

If Looks Could Kill

In between the darkness and light
flies the dreams of night.

Longing and pain tinge the sky
orange as the sun begins to rise
over the horizon,
killing the
star's bright glory.

Cloudy days always begin like this,
overcome by the rise
under the morning view I
look at you and see the stranger, the complete
danger of loving you.

Killing the star's bright glory
in the heavens we try to fly
like the birds, but we fall
like the dew.

In between....

Woes
owing
unlikely reunions
loving
dying

Being alive
enjoying every view.

Do you see the one that I see
every moment
as you tear apart the universe,
destroying all that you hold?

I see you
falling apart, outside my reach.

We are falling
over space and time, and
realize our love is
done
seeing delight in itself.

Colors whirl
over my vision
unskilled flailing
leads me closer to
death.

Keep everything here
in this little sphere.
Leave every regret;
let it fall back to the one who gave it away.

It can all go back!

Would you like to give it away?
Oh, to release the pain
under the bridge and
leave it there so you can
drive away with me.

But you walk away,
everyone always walks away (from me).

Desire twists my chest
enchantment
away with the moon that
descends to the dark side of the world.

Return to me
in dreams.
Go away
hot nightmare
troll.

Night brings the tears
overflowing - if your looks could kill I
would be dead right now.

Tenting in August

I'm tired,
beyond normal sleep,
or normal night visions.

I can't even daydream.

The clouds above hide
the meteor shower
from my eyes.
(I missed it again.)
My sigh hushes the crickets
for moments
then they forget I breathe.
(Or do I?)

The August dry grass
pricks my back and I
stare into heavenly moisture.
(Oh that I could evaporate and
rest so close to the stars.)

I allow myself to settle
to the bottom of the food chain,
ignoring the prick of mosquito
needles in my flesh.
Let them take what they wish,
I'll not linger long.

The dawn birds sing,
the clouds rush to dissolve somewhere else.
I fail to sleep another night,
just another among countless others.

As the pink dawn brushes my form
I begin to dream
of floating in the sky.

While a tree frog sings in my ear.

Statuette

The statues weep
in the garden of evil.
Their delta of devotions and
hungers
has stranded them in a wasteland.

Their marble cheeks gleam with beauty
in darkness or light.
They stand cold,
stubborn against all weather.
Their life of devotion to
heartbreak
holds a morbid allure.

2001

...I'm just a shadow...

Snowy Dreams

Diamond mountains
drift through the land.
Winter's breath touches
my hand.

I stare into the velvet sky,
but the wonders are lost to me.
Please take me away;
I don't want to stay
alone here.
Alone.

Gently, sweetly brush my face,
swirl so gracefully.
Float so softly through the sky,
'til you come to land!

Silver trees
reach for Eternity.
Moon's cool light
brushes the beauty.

I stare into the brightest star,
but the wonders are lost to me.
Please take me away,
I don't want to stay
alone here.
Alone.

Gently, sweetly sting my skin,
sway so softly by.
Float so slowly through the sky,
'til you come to land!

Mysti

I watch my breath
mingle with past,
playing with the fog
then fading with the sun.

I watch my sight
blur in the night
lids droop softly
tired from confusion.

I dream.
Yearning for that peace
and imagining loving arms
protecting me.

I'll Never Be

I can't see the horizon
life is blocking my view.
I don't know where my dreams are
they passed through me
to become sorrow, agony on my soul.
I can't see my colors
the sun is blocking my view.
I don't know what I'm made of
it all passes through me,
to become sorrow, agony on my soul.

When trust fades from existence,
the future slips through my hands.
When the night crowds closer
and hope trickles like sand
I say,
"I've given up, this is through,
I can't do this without you."

I'll never be
Complete.

Breath of Heaven

The morning sun warms my frozen skin,
barren thoughts fade with the moon.
Butterflies flit from bloom to bloom,
reminding me of angels in the sky.

Breath of Heaven,
touch me.
Lead me far from the shadow.
Breath of Heaven,
fly me higher,
far from the roots of the land

The evening song warms my every limb,
leaving me warm from deep within.
Birds warble songs of day's end,
bringing me back to my childhood.

Breath of Heaven,
free me.
Lead me to the memory.
Breath of Heaven,
bring me higher,
far from the sorrows of man.

Breath of Heaven,
touch me.
Lead me far from the shadow.
Breath of Heaven,
fly me higher,
far from the cruelties of land...
far from the sorrows of man...
far from the pain of my own hand.

Divided

First one step
then a thousand.
The miles divide until
we can't reach between them.

One moment,
one chance   one dream erased.

I gather my heart
and hold it before me
This love divides
my heart from my mind.

One dream
three words
left in me forever.

I cry silently as
the days draw me away,
but still I remember.

This regret,   this love,
will always remain the same.

Woe On You

You treat me like a mindless fool,

to cartwheel and perform.

You expect me to worship at your ugly feet,

delivering compliments you author.

The opinions you ask for

me to spout

are lies and filled with self-praise.

So when I deliver the truth,

your face clouds over

as you shout, then scream.

Woe on you

who tries to force your praises

from another's vocal cords.

Lonely, Silent, Sadness

The water's crash
rings through the air.
So silently
I sit and listen
to the sound of Lonely
and her tears
as they wash upon the shore.

So silently
the snowflakes fall.
Through the sky
they flit and flutter.
The sound of Silence
begins to swallow
any other thought.

Before the dawn begins to break
the thoughts of melancholy whirl
about the times that couldn't be.
While those that were seem meaningless
as I dance with Fear.
Lonely tears,
silent snowflakes
abound.

The wind's sigh
brushes the tree.
I sit and listen
to the sound of Sadness.
Her pains seem to breathe,
as they flow through the air.

After the Rain

The scent of the water soaked ground
seeps into my soul.
The lightning released,
this pain preceding the storm.

Far on my own
with nothing to hold,
doesn't seem bad at all
when I think of the chance
that I might not have touched you.

The rain pounded my fears into the ground
where they became one with dusky earth.
The sun making me complete
and the water rose to be consumed by the heat.
I watched the fog knowing my soul floated freely.

Your memory is still here,
and the pain still exists.
But you go on, and I must too.
I fought for so long,
trying to hold tight,
but wounded myself all the more.
The more that I grasped the harder you pulled away.

I remember stolen summer nights,
the fire so bright,
where you first said the words of love.

After the rain
my pain seems so far.
I dream that you see the same clouds,
and think of me.
Remembering.

Nature's Child

Laughing, she danced across the moonlit bridge,
reveling in the joy that swirled through every part of her being.
Becoming one with the night as she playfully dodged
through the shadows,
consumed by darkness
then bathed in light.

Her emotions are free here
without anyone to say what is proper for her
or anyone else.
She can rip away her swirling gown
leaving it to soak up the dew,
or she can wave her arms madly
without being told that she's possessed.

The sounds of the crickets,
the wind in the trees,
the water rushing beneath the bridge,
these are the only musicians she needs.

Made of Water and Earth,
she delights in dancing with her brothers
and sisters of the wild.

Returning to her origins
and soaking each movement and scent into her body,
she prepares for the days that she must move through the city
and be proper in Society's eyes.
But inside she'll always be the girl
who dances with nature
and sings with the breeze.

Pitch Black

The stars refuse to shine
the planets re-align,
this universe of dreams dissolves
into nothing once again.
The fog will rise to show
the sharp rays of love.

When dreams become reality
I awaken and cannot see
the truth within your lies.
I'm drowning in pain again.

Far from where we once began,
lost inside a barren land.
What's left of you and me
becomes the dust swirling in the wind.

Fallen on my own,
without your hand to hold.
I cry silently for you.

The stars refuse to shine,
the planets re-align,
this universe of loss expands
to consume all once again.
The fog rises to show
the wounds that should have faded.

I look at you
and what's left of me
as I'm tossed into a turquoise sea.
Left to sink deep into your past eternally.

The thought of love tears into me,
as you walk with her instead of me.
Leaving me among the thorns
of love's sweet rose.

Spirits of the Sun

Slipping over my skin
like warm honey.
Moving over my face
like the wind of the dawn.
Every caress golden,
each touch gentle.

Tearing over my skin
like wildfire.
Moving over my hands
like manacles they confine.
Every caress painful,
every cry in vain.

I cry out, torn between two lovers.
Either way I lose.

Blinded

Your breath mingles with mine,
side by side our souls burn as
we wander the same desert under flaming orbs.

The cool of night no longer soothes,
the rain cannot quench our thirsting.
Silence incurs more worth than gold,
peace untold.

Imagination dims as
we look through the eyes of the world.
No longer seeing the important,
just what we're told.

Revulsion

I can still feel you inside me,
pressing through my barriers.
You breech every security
making yourself at home.

I begin to breathe like a dragon
my flames searing you.
Metallic tears fall from your tainted eyes
as you plead for forgiveness.

I give it
though my shame begins to drown me.
My soul heaves and flickers
like a dying flame.

I can still feel you inside me,
observing my secrets.
You mock my healing
I become the victim
again.

I float in silence like the morning fog,

ignoring this chain that binds us.
I allow you to remain for if I didn't
I would be left alone
with this wretched self.

Strength

When the wind has teeth
and the stars freeze in the sky,
I'll join in the call of mourning.
When the stars plummet down,
only to shatter on the ground,
I'll be there to mold them back to glory.

When the dust rises high,
and the air starts getting thin
I'll join the clouds in graceful silence.
When the rain comes pouring down
only to bounce off the ground,
I'll be here to taste it on my tongue.

When time ceases to flow,
and my heart stills in my chest,
I'll join the voices of the dead with joy.
When my world tumbles down,
only to fade into the past,
I'll be peaceful in my knowing
that I was strong.

Blue to Green

The rain relieves the humid air,
as it pours in torrential emotion.
My backyard sighs as it drinks,
the birds cry with joy as they bathe.
I spin erratically, trying to catch every drop.

My soul, shriveled
I'm so thirsty.
I lust for things I cannot have
although I really don't want them.

The clouds parted.
The sun smiled.
A rainbow appeared just for me,
and I'm not thirsty anymore.

I am complete as the Son's rays
blend with the atmosphere,
turning blue to green.

Beyond Your Vision

Waging wars between myself and me.
Truthfully, these eyes can't see beyond
this vicious war inside.

These thousand voices
screaming to be heard,
are the remaining fragments
of my shadowed life.
They are all that's left
of the memories that were never retained.

Where is the prescription for my heart
that will pull away inflammation?
Where's the prescription that can mend the hurts
beyond your vision?

The stars float in an ocean of darkness
while I lose myself in this void.
These voices won't cease until they find their release.
I have the vision to know that won't come soon.

Please keep me whole!
Keep me safe from myself,
from these demons that can't be exorcised.
Where is the prescription that can mend the hurts
beyond your vision?

Nighttime Wishes

This star doesn't seem bright,
not as bright as it was.
The dream of the lifetime,
has fallen from me and
doesn't exist anymore.

I wish you well,
I wish you joy,
I wish the love you've found will stay,
this pain isn't for you,
it's mine.

The second of understanding isn't bright,
not like it was before.
When moments of happiness
pass with a flash
I cry in the dark alone.

I wish you here,
I wish you gone.

I wish you knew this love that I've found.
The fault is all mine, I ran out of time.

I was too scared to say the words.

My nighttime wishes haunt my dreams too,
where I can see you clearly.
The dreams of being in your arms
make it harder to wake.

The pain of wishes that will never come true,
tear my heart apart.

I wish you peace,
I wish you the joy
that you deserve all through your life.
This pain is for me,
it's mine.
I ran out of time.
I was too scared to say the words.

Reality Within the Dream

Forever I have waited.
Forever hasn't come.
Forever somehow dissipated,
as the night shoves past the sun.

Eternally it should have been,
but the meaning has been lost.
Now it's just me for you,
and you for yourself.

Forever could have been special,
a reality within the dream,
but here I stand
suffering.
You're nowhere to be seen.

Paper Angel Wings

Walking home,
feeling the pain of being torn.
This is just an ordinary day.

Hiding in this cave of night,
trying to imagine mistakes made right.
This is just an ordinary hour.

Flying too close to the ground,
makes the angel crash.
This is just an ordinary death.

You can't run
forever.
Once you fall,
you can't fly again.
You can't walk
to Heaven.
Your paper wings won't help you fly,
believe me I've tried.

Cool Mist

Lost along a dusty sidewalk,
far away from home.
Hiding from all the wandering eyes
that wish for me to fall.

Just another weary traveler,
searching for a cause.
Led to loud, crashing waves,
far from the valley green.

Standing with a million strangers,
the souls whom echo my own.
Our voices call out in silent greeting,
to the sunrise soon to come.

Hope seems to abound here,
where beauty can unfold.
Where violence is seen as grace,
and peace comes with the dawn.

Perhaps sometimes mermaids appear,
bringing dream orbs that wash away your fears.

Fantasy fades far from view,
driven away by the day.

Silence begets agony,
we die alone.

Far from home I wander,
searching for a dream.
The ocean understands my emotions,
and echoes them at my will.

Shadow

Loud voices
tumbling and raging,
stripping humanity away.
Tearing a hole in the silver lining,
destroying everything I want to hold.

Past nightmares
seething to frontal memory.
Revealing graves of my fragments
long since dead.
They rise and stalk my every breath,
seeking to destroy all I have left.

Body memories,
I remember your fingers tracing me.
You ground me slowly reducing me to nothing,
and the lessons are brought back when I see your eyes.
The threats are still clear
when I hear your voice.
Your touch still hurts
as you seek yet another hold,
so I lie still and say,

"I'm just a shadow,
        you cannot hurt me.
                You don't own me,
                        I don't remember."
                                I'm just a shadow."

New Beginnings

The blooms awaken,
brand new every morning.
The trees reach for the sky,
just like yesterday.

Where I am free,
in the sunrise,
floating on colors so pure.
Here I am free.
In the morning.
where I can begin again.

The winds blow fresh,
brand new every morning.
The birds sing their song,
just like yesterday.

I dance freely,
in the sunlight.
Floating on air so pure.

Here I am free
in the sunlight,
where I can begin again.

The darkness has no hold anymore.
Finally I can begin anew.

The stars wake again,
bringing a new phase of the moon.
Night blooms open their eyes,
while I shutter my own.

I dream a dance
in the sunlight.
Frolicking in the wind.
Here I am free
in dream sunlight,
where I can grow again.

Where I can bloom.

The Reason

I'm weak.
I hide behind these doors
refusing to see your face.
Pushing away the memories you create.
There's a reason they were forgotten,
the reason is here today.
I'm frail.
Drop me on the floor,
I'll shatter like a Fabergé egg.
Countless pieces without a way to mend.
There's a reason I lay broken,
the reason has your face.

I'm despised.
I look in the mirror, avoiding my own eyes.
These fears shouldn't have hidden behind this face.
There is the reason I lie broken.

2000

...I spin, so dizzy I can't see to the
tune of the crazymaker...

Darker Side

The music is dying
choked out
by the chains around my soul.
My mask molds hard,
cold
against my cheeks.
Pressing painfully against
my jaw.
Only slipping away
when I howl along with the four winds
alone in the dark.
Leaving me to wonder
if there's anything
left behind this plastic
or if it was smothered by my silence.
This vacuum deep within
threatens to suck me in
because my angel of mercy
has not descended from the sky.

Faith is hard to come by
even though I have
touched and seen all
it has to offer.
Instead, I am fading
becoming invisible,
and still, I delve deeper
exploring the darker side.
As the sun goes down it
leaves me plenty of shadows
in which to hide from

?

Garden

My poetry garden -
iron, raw, gorgeous language
crushes this burning, frantic monster
called, Pain.

Hollywood Perfection

When being a woman
doesn't seem to be perfection,
and the thrust of my breasts
or the pout of my lips
seem to need resurrection.
I am weak
and see fat instead of muscle.
When what's underneath is
allowed to dim
in comparison
to the outside package,
I open a magazine and
make notes on how to change.
How proud I am when I begin to
imitate Hollywood's "perfection"
without realizing my eyes are blind with
deception.
I forget my true
Perfection
by being just Woman.

The Red Pill

Secrets in my mind,
Threatening to break free.
Waiting for my time to bring
what I know lies ahead.

Nightmares on the table,
dreams strewn on the floor.
Hopes of what was going to be,
are not here anymore.

Dreams change,
then fade behind my eyes.
As the days fly,
it's not easy on my mind.
Somehow, I saw it come to this
in the visions I'm allowed.
My heart changes so fast but
sunrise and sunset look the same.

Nightmares stalk the halls,
your voice floods my head.
Guilt and pain blend into me,
my power fades from view.

Crow calls from the sky,
your voice harsh in my ears.
I know that I'm already dead,
the power is in your hands.

But no matter how I try to fly,
you always pass me by.

Not So Sorry Anymore

So confused, even more than before
only now I think I'm all wrong.

So long I've choked my pain,
goodbye is too hard to say.
Spiritual tears will hopefully fade.
(Don't want to let go,
the road's become unknown.)

The pain on your face so clearly said,
you can't believe these words come from me,
yet I keep reciting hurts
as if I have something to prove.

You seem to think that I would lie,
and you erase your love as I cry.
I'm not sorry that I'm hurting you.
These wounds won't hide anymore.

Walk With Me

Song on repeat
depression complete.
Finding it hard to breathe,
walk with me and maybe...
Eyes red, burning from acid tears.
Wallowing in the misery
of one more failure.
Walk with me and maybe...

Hair limp, skin pale
I hide, alone with my cares.
Not revealing that I am frail
walk with me and maybe...

Insanity seems so near,
disillusionment aesthetically calms my fear.
The rhyme and the reasons are missing,
faded as the stars fade from the day.

Walk with me and maybe
my crystal sorrow
will be shattered beyond repair.

Snowflakes and Secrets

I like the silent hush of winter,
the cold numbs my being.
The gentle crush of my boots is hardly noticed,
but the hunter can easily follow.

Mingling

The brutal, humid wind
undulates fiercely,
pushing all in its path into agonized writhing.

Grass reacts like water of the Dead Sea
the trees bend over, branches wrapping around trunks
as in grief.
South winds push against North,
North against South,
moist Air wins and carries clouds on her breath.

Scents of heat and melting tar
choke cleanliness from my lungs.
I gasp and writhe with nature
our screams mingle into one.

Chasm

The leaves swoop dejectedly,
as my heart plummets to the ground.
The rain drizzles silently,
like the tears on my face.

Wandered from the path we began,
we stand in the cold.
Bared to the elements,
we drown then we burn.

The clouds rumble and shake,
the earth begins quake.
I scream and I yearn as I watch all of nature
pull you away.

I drown in the fear of losing
the last thing I know.
You live near, but so silently,
I try to ignore this hole.

Far from where we began,
without the sight of land.
I scream and I call, I can see you
but you can't see me standing here.

My calls bounce off the hills,
and echo in my ears.
The pain grows and radiates,
you're so close, yet so far.

These emotions take me over,
until my being goes numb with the longing
to feel you near me.

I want to touch your spirit...

Secondary Emotional Blather

Why does triumph fade away after confrontation?
Why do I fear the pieces of my broken heart
even as they mend again?
I prefer to cry in the dark and feel alone,
in place of feeling peace and light knowing my form.

Small hesitations seem so large,
large hesitations crush my soul.
Far from home, lost in the storm,
sad memories of Yesterday keep me gathering
the pieces of my shattered heart.
Once upon a time, so long that it's forgotten
belief has faded just the same.
Waiting for you to walk away,
then I do it myself, afraid of being abandoned.

Try loving me like I love me,
and nothing will last.
Try loving me like you love me,
and I might let you in.
Keep feeling like you do,
and I may learn to feel.
Try talking and I may regain my ears.

Let me learn to love me,
as you learn along.
Let me alone when I ask,
and push no farther than I allow.
Tear my walls down gently,
without my knowledge.
Drown my sorrows with me,
in a bottle of wine
until only you are known.
Then let's forget my moments of feeling
until I do again.

Near

Smooth, yet sad beauty
beneath white winter bed
dream forest rose
the Spring sun shines near
pink Summer's night
dawns near.

CrazyMaker

It's done.
I've lost myself again.
My suicidal drop ended
as the whirlpool opened its hungry maw.
Soul, spirit, will, mind
consumed
by the hated emotions you create with pride.
I fell from my cloud above,
forgetting my lack of will.
I spin, so dizzy I can't see,
to the tune of the CrazyMaker.

Darker Than Sin

I am bottomless
beyond understanding.
I am like time,
without hesitation.
Only when we're far apart,
does the cold seem so much sharper
(maybe these bones are getting old).
My fantasies are dusty,
packed in some old trunk.
Only on my secret adventures does the lock break,
letting me feel free.
I am bottomless,
darker than your sin.
I am like time ...
without hesitation.

Ashes

When fancy feelings scattered
Constructing memories of shadow
Quick and frenzied disdains
Maim.

Hide and Run

When did I begin to play this game?
Run and hide.
Where did I begin to see myself as prey?
Hide and run away.
I try to go back,
but I can't repaint the past.

The sun shines on my head,
the tears fall into dust.
Pain seems older than time,
Denial's wine has run dry.
Stark reality burns,
hated fire.

Forgotten Betrayal

Roses engraved in copper,
created by a master's hand.
The master gone without a whisper,
the rose hidden behind dark wood.
The creator losing the vision,
the vision deemed trivial.
A betrayal loud and blatant,
but forgotten without care.

Guilt Ridden

The scent of you is fading;
the feel of you is gone.
I move forward
as you fall into the past's hole.
And I wonder
how it felt
to be loved by you.

The sound of your voice
rarely enters my dreams.
Your sweet caress,
never hushes my screams.
The present moves onward
and drags me along
leaving you in Memory's black hole.

The guilt I feel for
letting you go,
never hesitates to let me know
my love for you must not have been strong enough
to keep you from the past.

Plaintive Whisper

Kiss this delicious dream.
Watch the beauty
of the sky's moon.
Ache after all has faded.
Whisper plaintively,
"return".
Taste the delicious vision,
as the day lives.
Cry with joy as night
breathes anew.

When Evening Comes

When the sweet summer wind begins to blow,
the trees bow down low,
asking for this dance.
Their branches weave peace in gentle motions.

The stars twinkle on the dew covered grass,
the silence washes over me.
And the peace of the evening,
soothes my soul like a balm.

Your smile flashes in my memory,
pain is left behind,
only joy remains.
I remember once upon a time,
when my prince rode a strong steed.

The leaves move with the wind,
gently reminding this heart
while the storms come and go,
it is my love that stays the same.

From the past I move forward,
into a future without you by my side.
I know that you will love her more
than I,
but I set you free.
Free to be hers, and she yours.

Faith

Overwhelming, tearing pain
rips through my shattered soul
as you pray for healing
in your humble body.
Burning, aching pain
scalds my eyes.
I yearn for tears
as I realize
you have something
I have never known...
faith
in the One above.

Night Kills the Day

Towering masses
of angry, red flame.
Blazing fingers
placing the blame.
Raw anger traded,
emotional waves we ride.
Like the earth and a comet,
our masses collide.

I am the dark,
you are the light.
You try to destroy
me by being
jealous of my rule.

With your ego
flying high,
you lie
and declare you're letting me go.
But any existence
should know
that it is I who walked away.

After all,
the day can't own the night,
and you can't free what you've never held.

Now I have won,
my soul's intact.
I leave you with the guilty knowledge
of having become a scar
upon my soul.

You never had me, so you can't let me go.

Thunderbolt of Desire

For Ash

When frenzied passion sweeps across my heart
a deliciously searing thunderbolt of desire
fragments the pulse.

Scattered flame warming feelings and disdains.

Quick fire found soft,
sting tempered tranquil by the shadow.
Silky ashes imprinting the pyre.

Skeleton in the Closet

You say you know me
but the knowledge is over your head.
I drown in oceans that you'll never understand.
Your eyes are so focused on things above
that you can't see the storm of your creation.

Words of Hell and Damnation
coat your lips.
Looks of Hate and Condemnation
radiate from your eyes.
Fake tears and prayers
spew from your every orifice.

My heart is the dust at your feet.
My tears flavor your bitter tea.
My soul is heaped upon your head.
My dreams are buried in your yard.
There is nothing left of me but broken bones.

I lay here,
only to rise at night.
Young I am supposed to be - old I have become.
Tears and screams are my only companions
in this dark enclosure.

Stumbling Blocks

Reality is slipping
time is slowly ticking.
Today turns into forever
as I feel sorry for myself,
because security was never a wealth.

Wandering free
at least that's the way it used to be.
Just Me, and Me, and Me.
Serving myself without eyes to see
the needs around.

Lost
strayed too far from the truth.
Having forgotten the cost
of following Freedom's lurid tone.

Wolf Brother

For Sam

Snatch me up,
carry me away,
cover me with a pelt of gray.
Run beside me,
wild and free,
forgetting anything ever was
or ever will be.

Together
let's be the hunters instead
of the hunted.
Let's greet the moon
with harmonious howls,
as we rule the night
with our strength, speed, and courage.

Brought together

without accident.
Ashes in the wind
caught by a gentle paw.
Slowly reformed,
by her brother wolf.

Run beside me,
wild and free.
I need you, please need me.

<u>Despondency</u>

I stare at the rain that
touches crimson leaves reverently.
I long for such a touch as the
rain continues mockingly.

I scream until my spirit bleeds,
the wind pushes my cries away,
Eyes weep, soul flailing in the grasp
burning trails upon my marble cheeks.

Seconds pass me by so hastily,
years feel like a hazy dream.
Misery invades my heart,
as I kiss you goodbye eternally.

I cry, "Inside my spirit bleeds,"
as I am driven to my knees.
Gravity won't let me free,
I'm weighted by despondency.

Love Changed Quickly

This song makes me think of you.

Remembering your warmth only makes me grow colder.

The snowflakes pierce my skin,

like a million needles.

The wind numbs my back

with its massage.

I go from loving you because you were here;

to hating you because you're not.

Crying myself to sleep

knowing I'll never know love as real

as yours.

Waking in warm sunlight

then reaching for you. . .

remembering you're gone.

Living in pain,

as I watch lovers play along the beach.

Starting all over again,

life will never be the same.

Cold Whispers

Higher than the purple clouds I climb,
until I cannot be touched by time.
Reality doesn't matter, the wounds on my soul can heal.
I can fly free

Closer to the sun I fly,
until my flesh merges with the heat.
Body doesn't matter, it's only a way to be.
Finally, I can fly free.

Without pain, without the past
surely goodness and mercy will last.
Without fear, without tears,
surely weightlessness and purity won't pass.

Into the galaxy I explore,
calling every star by name.
Gravity doesn't matter, the shackles broken free,
release is sweet upon the air.

When I awake, I see your face
and I return to that old, barren hovel.
Where my life is yours, and my soul watches so cold
whispering the way of freedom

Gravity Lost

me

   take

      stars

         and

            moon

               the

                  outwards

                     and

                        Upwards

Silvered

Wind
 bending and twisting,
whispering against grassy hills.
Sounds are silky and
peace shimmers
through the silver heavens.

Act of Release

Nothing will ever bring you back,
this I know.
It is past time for me to let go.
My soul is heavy,
my heart is rotting
from this pain.
Agony intensified a hundred-fold,
so tightly I grasp and cling.
Easier is the act of release,
harder the act of restraint and denial.
The time for you has come,
and passed,
you are deep within what was.
I should have known such perfection
wouldn't last.
The breath of your life whispers so softly,
I have to strain to feel your life's touch.
So many have forgotten,
their lives remain unchanged by your essence

Your beauty.
Your words.
Your pain.
You become only yesterday
as I deliver the last blow,
and unfurl my hand.
Leaving you where you should be,
but holding you   deep in my memory.

Wounded Waltz

Feeling countless silvered memories
heaving in
Frost's wounded waltz.
In unaccustomed soul spaces
the lover's conversation
a ghostly whisper.

Velocity

This minor ache of
emptiness
deepens into a yawning cavity
as I pull away
from life yet again.
Hiding as I lick the wounds
that ooze with venom.
You used your words
with terminal velocity,
wounding me.
Like sticks and stones, they
bruise and break,
while you autograph my heart
with a pen dipped in poison.
Smiley face mocking me
eyes cruel,
mouth twisted,
mirroring your own.
This moment reminds me of all
I'll never have,
because I'm frozen to the bone.

Cold Melancholy

The sounds of melancholy
swirl around me.
They reach out,
clawed hands demanding
my participation
in the center of their circle.
Timeless sounds of melancholy
linger in the dense fog
that only rain can pierce
in its suicidal drop from hierarchy.
Not even my will to be free
can clear a path for my passing.

Trapped

This flame isn't as bright
as it once was.
This night
is darker than ever.
One step forward,
I crash into a wall
once erected
to keep the ultraviolet rays
at bay.

Prisoner of my own
architecture,
soundproof walls
toss my cries
back at me.

Exorcism

I remove the offending dirt
from beneath my fingernails,
trying to remove
your dirt from my mind
with the same efficiency.
I only remember
more vividly.

I pretend I'm brushing you away
with each stroke
of the comb,
pulling each strand
from entanglement.
I can't imagine
detangling lies.

I've become the proverbial fool
as I return to you
the next day.
Allowing you to push
and pull me,
causing never-ending pain.
Small manipulations,
brought to higher elevations,
feels like a horror movie
when you're near.
But I'm weak,
and somehow believe
I need you.
So, I'll clean my nails,
brush my hair,
cry myself to sleep,
and see you tomorrow.

Dusk Till Dawn

My voice is slowly fading
into the back of beyond.
No one ever warned me
that I'd be rendered mute
if I carried on.

Hope is slowly dying,
crushed in a giant's hold.
But I wouldn't dream of complaining,
pain should go on
untold.

Time is leaving me behind,
amidst the bones
I'm chewing on the rind
while you eat the fruit
of my failure.

The air fills my lungs with poison
while you flourish, so clean.
Why doesn't life succumb to the repulsion
of loving the vampire
instead of the victim?

Retreat...back,
I've lost another
and I'm wounded.
Pull away from the light,
I'm not worthy
to walk with the living.
I'll bleed alone.

From dusk till dawn
and then I'm gone.
I never even stood here.

Little Princess Girl

Little girl lost in deep thoughts.
Little princess lost inside her crown.
Tiny shoe, missing its mate,
soulful eyes missing life.
Silent years come bursting forth,
a volcano of emotions, red hot,
ready for your destruction.
Everything I've become,
earthy or not,
floating through space.

1999

...Tears release as I scrub
you from my skin...

Closer to Healing

For Andrew

The hurt threatens to
rob me of my will.
The pain entices me
to stand still.

But when I turn to you,
you say, "let it go."
And your words draw me closer to healing
than you will ever know.

Simple words
said in sympathy
reminds me that someone cares
and understands.

And I whisper,
"Never leave me,
don't forsake me,
never close the door.
I need you more than my words
could ever say."

And when you
take me in your arms
the world around me fades,
while you whisper in soft reassurance
that you will always care.

And your words draw me closer to healing
than you will ever know.

The Fortress

It seems that I am forever sinking.
I feel the shadows crowd closer,
the clouds are blocking
the beautiful warmth of the sun

Noxious fumes rob my breath, and sting my eyes,
shrill screams pierce my head from birds in the skies.
Fear and rumors rob me of my will.
Storms and shadows plunder me until I am still.

I curl into a ball,
seeking to protect my vital organs.
I futilely hope that the attacks will cease,
but they don't
               so I build walls around.

An impenetrable fortress stands,
surrounded by a moat of acid.
A solitary princess dwells therein,
and not even the bravest of princes
               dares venture forth.

Clouds of darkness hover over,
long spikes protrude from the walls.
Frigid wind whips all around,
echoing the cries of mourning from within.

Not a note of song from the fife,
nor the giggles of a child.
Not a whisper of laughter or peace,
not one glint of love.
Just sorrow
        mourning
                and defense

Sometimes
passersby see the form of a woman.
Large brown eyes are said to gaze from her pale face.
She seems to be searching for some sign of her knight,
but all she sees is the remains of him impaled on a spike.

The castle she built for her protection
became the destruction of his love,
Her absolute sorrow.

Frozen World

Frost,
white, restricting
growth.
Burning cold
rapes this flower
that flourished brilliantly
in the sun.

Winter is coming.
The soul mourns
her loss of
glorious brother, Sun.

Darkness descends.
Cold wind,
frigid ice
drives the soul
deeper
into the warmth of itself.

Pray Spring, do come,
else all will perish.

<u>Fragile Time</u>

Time.
Beautiful,
shimmering
like aqua colored water
contained by banks,
yet still left to wander
and trickle
through everything.
Hidden,
pure
until I rush to meet it
and try to catch it.
Not realizing
that to hold time
is like catching
a snowflake
in the palm of my hand,
and expecting it
to stay intact.
Unchanged by the heat
                    of my existence

Lost Soul

Ashes to ashes,
dust to dust,
the end of life.
The circle
will never be broken,
one must live,   one must die.

But if the heart leaves
before its time...
But if the body lives
long after the will is gone...

Soot stains my face,
burns cover my body.
Somehow, I came out alive,
but I'm destroyed.
Only pain remains.

Ashes to ashes,
dust to dust,
that is all that remains.
Only Ashes is here now,
the past is behind,
but the pulling of scars remains.

Constellation

Lost,
forever to me.
Far beyond,
my mortal eyes can see.
You gaze into the sun,
as I stare at the moon.
You're so far away.

Soul,
thrown into the stars.
Not letting us,
forget who you are.
But the sunset holds no beauty,
the rain only echoes my tears.
You're too far away.

Even the winds call out for you.
All of nature weeps along with me.
All the world gazes at your image in the stars,
trying to pull you back into our arms,
but you're too far away.

Forward

I say that I don't care
more often than not
It's hard for me to share
what my heart and soul are feeling
So I dare to hide it away
and prepare myself for a futuristic fall

Your insults ring in my ears
all the day long
I turn away to hide my tears
I won't reveal that I am weak
I suffer on my own
And prepare myself for the casting of another stone

I don't know where I'm going
I don't know where I'm from
I've been taught that I'm worth nothing
I've been used more than loved
I pray that I'll live to see tomorrow
And that I'll be able to stand
I don't know where I'm going
but I'm leaving this behind.

Give Me Death

Hand me death
on a silver platter
and let me be the feast
Let me surrender
This soul
leaving the body behind.

Give me death
in a copper goblet
that I may drink deeply
It would never be as bitter
as the one I choked on
the day you died
because of my foolish risk

Just give me death,
or let me leave this torment
at the feet of God.

Understanding's Seduction

I am bleeding
Deep
Deep
Deep
No one sees but you
who consumes me.

You still the Amazon with three words
                (I love you)
Then bring out the kitten in one sweet touch
                (Be still, my love)
How tempting
To throw fear to the wind
How damning
I know it is
How easily
You carve your name on my heart.
How swiftly
Promises fall from my lips.

I am so terrified that I will hurt you,
But I haven't the strength
To stop
Your seductive understanding.

Rebirth

Spring is here,
I hear her song.
The wind sings through the trees,
the leaves burst forth.

Spring is here,
I hear her minstrels
Glorious birds all shapes and colors
blend their songs in perfect harmony.

I turn my face to the breeze
And close my eyes
Basking in the glory of a new season
A new birth
All things fresh, young, and pure
Where even the heart and soul can be reborn.

Splinter

This knowledge
that you will never
kiss
hold
comfort
adore
shield
soothe
me
digs into my skin
a splinter
traveling through my veins until
thrust deep my heart
causing constant
agony
reminding always
that you will never
touch me again
in any way.

Going On

Lost
In ever darkening shadows
Tossed
By never ending storms
Wandering
Seeming alone
Wondering
What I can call my own

Destroyed
Putting together all the pieces
Void
Emotions forever wrong
Fighting
For what belongs to me
Wanting something more

Fearing that fear will destroy me
Fearing the fate that will befall me
Fearing myself
Fighting myself
But I'll keep going on.

Prey

If the eyes are the windows to one's soul
　　　What are yours saying to me?
You are so gentle and loving,
　　　But your eyes tell me nothing.
They are empty and cold,
　　　They are the eyes of the old.

I try to speak,
　　　But you smother me with kisses.
You stand up for me
　　　You hold me
　　　　　You're always here
But your eyes say nothing

You act like I'm a possession
　　　But yet you don't own me
You treat me like I may melt,
　　　But you don't shield me from doubt.
My fairytale picture of you is fading
　　　And confusion reigns.
I meet your cold eyes,
　　　Maybe it's time we walked different paths
　　　Or maybe we always did.

Lost You

I cried for you
for the first time
sobbing out my grief
mourning
that you missed
last night's sunset
missed
hearing the thunder
and catching the rain on your tongue.

I cried for me
for the first time
healing
some old wounds
mourning
that I missed
a million smiles
missed
feeling your caress
and the look of love in your eyes.

I cried for us
for the first time
letting
my anguish
take control
mourning   lost days
lost seconds   lost life.

Testament

Finally
my voice has strength
and thank God,
else I would be dead.

My voice box
was ripped from
this body
as a testament to your strength,
but you never thought
to ban the pen and paper
from my hand.
And there
in bold black
on pure white paper
I tell my story.

My voice,
the testament of your
lies and hate,
that I will leave behind
as a testament -
your legacy.

Pain vs. Love

We stand so close,
and I hold his hand,
but he's so far away
and I don't understand.

I see his death through his eyes
he feels I can destroy him
but only love can heal....doesn't it?

I press my face into his jacket,
as he holds me close and all I hold is his blanket.

He'll leave me soon
body along with mind
It's only a matter of time.
It's happened before.

I love him
I try to say in word and deed,
but his eyes and ears are shielded.
His pain reigns his every day
and I cannot compete.

Still Standing

Just because you're ignoring me,
doesn't mean I'm not here.
I'm not going to flee,
I haven't any fear

           anymore

You tried to burn me down,
reduce me to ashes,
but I refused to melt down
from the lightning's searing lashes

Crying and sighing
didn't get me anywhere.
Destroying and lying,
you refused to play fair.
Despite you I became strong
and pulled from your hold.
Your deception didn't last for long,
now you're the one standing in the cold.

After the onslaught,
I'm still standing.
After the lies you wrought,
I'm still standing.
I'm stronger than you thought I was,
I'm the victor not your slave because
survival

        is its own act of rebellion.

Witch on Hopper's Lane

For so long this darker voice
has been so quiet,
now it screams once more
all the anger and frustration I feel
urging me to cry in a never-ending scream
begging me to never fall silent again
fighting to keep me from falling into that damned
well of self-pity once more.
It reminds me that I am an island unto myself,
that I am queen of an evil kingdom
while my heart knows it's not true.
But instead of fighting
I give in
to the urge of this darkness
allowing this fear to dictate
what I show to others.
Making me an Emmy nominee, without acting on the screen.
Dare not show this softer side
that loves to be cuddled
that loves white kitty kats with blue, satin eyes.

This softer woman that looks better in white
than unforgiving black
but the rejection of this person
that is so obviously me
keeps my soft side hidden under this layer of black cloak.
And I remain the crazy witch lady of Hopper's Lane

Nightmare

"No!"
I scream as I sit up in bed
"Go away!" I please as I grasp my head
Horror of the awful dream washes over me
Terror clings to my back
Man shouting...screaming...vanishing
All that's left behind is the stench of death
Recoiling from the truth as I realize
Everything revealed will come to pass.

Galaxy of You

The galaxy is in your eyes,
every constellation, planet, and star.
I see them all,
perfect and beautiful.
Cradled there for all time,
without savage mists to cloud their splendor.
Glimmering and shining,
black holes hinting in the distance.
Your eyes are your truth,
nothing is hidden
not even your blemishes
I love you for your beauty
And for your shades of darkness.

Lake Peace

The need to write,
so very strong.
The yearning to reach out,
eats my innards.
The need to speak,
aches in my throat.

But alas,
no words spring from my pen.
No hateful thoughts explode in my mind.
All I feel,
and know in perfect clarity,
is peace.

I am the oak log
that floats gently in the water.
lap, lap, lap,
the gentle waves caress my body.
The water catches me
and gently hold my feet from the
sharp rocks below.

My skin begins to wrinkle,
and my fingers have shriveled like prunes.
So with a sigh I wade out of the lake,

and stretch out on the shore.

Listening to the waves
and lake animals sing their songs.
I smell the damp earth,
and breathe it in deeply.

Now my time for rest is over,
I look up at the steep path leading
away from my sanctuary.
The time is now,
for me to return to harsh life.

I close my eyes
and commit the smells and sounds of peace
to my memory.
Then I return to
your reality.

Shower in the Dark

Lights off
water on
sheer bliss
as
the water pounds
against my flesh
massaging
lingering aches
away

Behind closed door
locked away
from the world
finally
tears release
cleansing my soul
as
I scrub you
from my skin
but don't succeed
in shoving you from my mind.

I.C.U.

I clutch your hand,
tight between mine
and watch you
fearful
of the possibility of death.

Will the Light steal you away?

Intensive pain
rips through me
as I press your hand to my lips.
Allowing aqueous tears
to create paths of sorrow

Will you wake after this sleep?

In I.C.U.
Hope dripping away
In time with your I.V.
ICU as nothing but alive.
It's killing me to let you go
Still, you fade away.

Intertwined

Emotion

    Foreign

        Ache

           Screaming

               "Know me!"

Tearing

    Tears

        From

           My

               Weary eyes.

Love's

    Lost

        Forever

           Name

               Far beyond

Light

    Gone

        Life's

           With

               The night's

Forever
     Without
        Precious
           Love's
               Warm embrace
Away
     Pain
       Lie
          Dreaming
              Of freedom.

One Second

For one second
peace calmed my heart
as I put
your words
aside
with your disturbing deeds

For one second
Love graced his face
as he looked
into my
eyes.
I thought all would be well,
until he walked away

If only
one second
was
one lifetime,
 content I would be.

Perfect Night

Surrounded by pieces of my shattered self,
I live in the darkness,
loving endless night.
The moon shines upon me,
cool and bright
protecting me from harsh daylight.

The whole world is sleeping, that's how it seems.
Alone in the darkness,
dreaming my dreams.
Silence surrounds me
and holds me tight.
For a while
everything seems perfectly right.

Spring Sunset

The sky's glory and splendor
      are constantly changing
Intricate colors and dazzling patterns
      spread with careless abandon

I long for the glory and splendor
      of myself
I ache for the patterns and colors of my soul
      to be revealed with abandon
I yearn to be free
      without restraint
I wish to reveal myself
      with the intricate patterns of the sky

The stars reveal themselves in endless glory
I sleep with a smile
      dreaming of my hidden sunset.

The Dreame

Such warm
Comforting
Solace
Your arms surround me
Kisses rain on my face
You hold me tight
Rocking me to sleep
When I reach out
The sunlight slaps my face
You are gone
Never there
You haven't been for years

Forever With You

On a cloudy day You walked into my life
offering me security, You said everything would be all right
Can I trust my heart to You?
You could wipe my tears away...
Should I give my heart to You?
You promise that You will stay...
I took the deepest look into Your eyes,
and I saw truth and clarity, no lies.
I may walk into forever with You.

I'm so confused, I just don't know,
but a voice whispers that You won't let go.
Should I give my heart to You?
You promised You will always stay...
Should I give my heart to You?
You can soothe all this pain away...
I take one long look deep into Your eyes,
And I see truth and love instead of lies
I'll think I'll gaze into forever by Your side.
I'll walk into forever with You.

Embracing the Storm

The clouds are closing in,
rain threatening to fall.
I balance precariously on this cliff,
waiting patiently for the storm.
For I am strong,
           and it cannot move me.

I close my eyes
lifting my arms and head.
Embracing the rain and wind
I wait the storm out

Driving rain
thundering clouds,
lightning aimed at my head
Pounding hail,
whispering fears,
winds that push me around.
I just stand strong.
           I'm stronger than your storm.

Blood Moon

From my bed of daisies
you drag me.
Pulling me higher and higher
into the sky.

You toss me at your feet
on a blood red
crescent moon.
I cower
As you point out every failure,
and convince me
that I am nothing.
Little by little,
you bleed me to death.
My blood absorbed greedily by the moon rock
to join the crimson river.
Then for good measure,
just to make sure that I'll never stand again,
you lift me high
and throw me on the tip
of the moon,
impaling me.

When you leave
I stare
down
down
down
At the world I can never rejoin.

Ice Queen

She lives on an island of ice,
her heart is dust in its coffin.
Her castle floats far into the ocean,
from which there isn't sight of land.

Silver tears are frozen to her cheeks,
And her skin is cold to the touch.
Her eyes are blinding cold, empty,
her breath is the night's frost.

From her breast she cut her heart
and placed it in an ice coffin
She cried her last tears of failure and pain
Where they froze upon her cheeks.

Her eyes are glazed over
and she watches the world from afar
She has accepted this as her fate,
to life she will never return.
For she is dead – frozen and no more.

Fathomless & Falling

Tears
forming behind my eyes
   but they don't fall
     I've forgotten how to let go.

Hurts
inflicted by your lies
   I try to stand tall
     but my eyes betray me

Tears
relived in the night
   uncertainties and worries dance around
     wailing for attention they already have

Mirrors
reveal my soul in their reflected light
   she shimmers like a ghost
     eyes fathomless, empty of the tears that wish to flow

Falling
through endless space
   you stand back and watch
     I close my eyes
            just let yourself go...

X Marks the Spot

Miles
we traveled
through the flame.
Hand in hand
each step in time.

Searching for the treasure on the map,
but the X kept moving.

Miles
we traveled
through the ice.
Hands kept busy,
feet out of step

I don't understand as you hand me the map,
until you walk out of sight.

Map so wretched,
burnt by the flame.
Red, orange, yellow
choked by ice.

And X stopped moving.

X marks the spot where you last stood.

The treasure lost forever.
Who is to blame?

Velvet Lover

He surrounds me,
dark and comforting.
I breathe in his scent,
and open my arms to embrace him.
His wind caresses my body,
And he gently dries my tears.

Its black, velvet hands caress my throat
Gently without threat
Its sister traces glimmering paths
That are safe to tread upon
Its brother hides me
Form evil and from light
My spirit springs forth
And I dance with all my might

I lick my lips
And taste his essence.
I fall back into comforting arms
and sleep.

When I wake
I find myself burnt and destroyed
by the enemy
I hide in the shade
and wait
for my gentle lover to return;
to tend my wounds
and show me peace.

<u>Dismay</u>

You come to me
on the wings of a bird
you hold me close
oh tenderly
then make your request
"Avenge me, love."
But oh I grieve
for I know not how.

My Heart Overflows

My heart overflows with peace!
The gentle wind pushes the storm away,
leaving me free and strong.
Contentment reigning,
eyes revealing my true self.

My heart overflows with joy!
The sun pushes the night away,
leaving me green and blooming.
Hope reigning,
eyes kind and gentle.

My heart overflows with love!
You pushed the hate away,
leaving me open to You,
Affection reigning,
eyes gazing openly into Yours.

You pushed my pain away,
leaving me open and caring.
My heart is awake,
and I'm ready to choose life.

Eternal Rest

I am so tired
So old
So ready for death,
Eternal rest

So exhausted
My power weak
Soul drained
My aura
Faded

Blissful nothing
Waits somewhere
Beyond this
Madness

That I could
Rush toward
Death
With my own hand
Means nothing to me
For I want to leave
As I have come.

Destruction Into Singing

My joy is like the waterfall,
overflowing and bountiful,
singing its loud and graceful song.

I go to my hidden place
  Behind the liquid curtain
   and lose my Self
     within myself

I know who I am
and it baffles me.
I had never hoped to understand.
This web had tangled all around me,
and left to me no mercies

But here I stand.
listening to my soul's song
of freedom, perhaps even worth.
I've been pulled free
of violent, destructive seas.
My hopelessness has turned to joy,
and my joy into a waterfall.

The Red Glass

The shattered pieces of my life,
lay on the floor before me.
Some sharp that bring blood to the touch,
others dull and small
never to be found again.
How could I let you break me?
Now it's too late, there's no remedy.

I've gathered the scattered pieces,
and locked them away.
They sit gathering dust,
waiting for the day I have the courage
to piece them together.
Silent tears caress my heart,
how will I ever begin to start?

Fragments   memories never remembered again.
Pieces   of a past best left forgotten
Words   that left my heart an empty shell
Emotions   raw and left guiding my way

Blood warm tears,   fallen because of you.

<u>Flight</u>

Fly into the mountains
Lay down your head
Rest
Your pain is over

Fly into the heavens
Perch on a star
And
Watch over

Soar beyond imagination
Visit my dreams
As
You pass over

Kiss me though
It is temptation
I want to with you
But
My time's not over

Though I'll miss you
Cry and grieve
I send me love to you
As you take your leave

Fly into the heavens
Perch on a star
And
Watch over me
Soar beyond imagination
Visit my dreams
As
You pass over
Kiss me though
It's
Temptation
I want to go with you...
I send me love with you
As you take your leave.

Bloody War

Headache
Throbbing
Your distorted face
Blurs
As you rant
And rave
Pulling down
My protection
With every syllable
Making me
Vulnerable
Naked

Crying
My war-torn heart
Aches
As you point
And accuse
Blocking ears
I try to
Reconstruct the great wall
I wave the white flag
But still, you attack

Oh, I wish for an
Armistice
At the very least.

Body Snatcher

The story of my life
is almost at the end,
or so I fear.
The hairs on my neck
quiver
sensing danger is near.
This death will be violent
not peaceful and painless.
This death with come slowly
as I become an
unwilling organ donor.

It is not enough
that you have my heart.
You want everything
even if you have to steal it.
Piece by piece
you'll cut everything from me,
until only bleached bone remains.

But your magic bottle can't hold my soul.

Foolish, Cold Woman

For so long I have been walking through this maze
That I don't know how to begin again
My breadcrumbs have long since fallen from my hand
And the birds follow close behind seeking the last crumb.
For so long I have been on my own
That I don't recognize a face that cares
And I don't care to confide
Because I'm wounded
And trust has its price.
Dark
Cold
Impartial woman.

For so long I have been locked in this castle
Left to wander aimlessly
Searching for the fabled secret exit
For so long I have been hungry for something I cannot name
And no matter how I eat
I cannot fill the void.

I am weak - I want strength.
I am strong - with self-pity.
I am trapped by you
Or
Am I trapped by me?
I cannot remember.
I felt you lay the first brick
And I set my concrete heart
Inside the cornerstone.
So we both have won.
You rid yourself of me
Bruised
Raped
Trivial woman.
I have laid my heart to rest.
Empty
Cold   Impartial
W
O
M
A
N

Scraps of Love

Close my eyes
Try to sleep
Block out anger
Into sleep retreat
From
Glued on smiles
Confetti love
Beautiful only
When floating above

Pain so deep
Lightning anger
Into my precious
Dreams you wander
Grim Reaper
Sent to harvest
My heart
Shrinking back as I hear your laughter

Cry no tears
In your presence
Glue on smile
Shield my pain
From
You who thrives upon it

Internal bleeding
Kills me slowly
As
Confetti falls
Upon my head

Life - Life = ?

I reveal my pain without shame,
refusing to believe that I'm insane.
I vent my feelings with each violent stroke of the pen
Or letting the typewriter hammer
each letter onto the page with brute strength.
I am anger, pain, despair
hear me cry out.
Let not your ears drown out each cry of pain
you are not blind,
And in this way, I will reach you.
I will reach out and grab you
with the violence of syllables,
without thought for your feelings or response.
I am tired, angry, overwhelmed
hear me scream.
You wear sunscreen to try and block the rays of my pain
but no SPF can block it
You wear sunglasses to try and reduce the glare
but no tint can decrease this anger's light
Welcome to my island
Where all pain imagined or real is multiplied
By 5,000
Where thought and reason mean nothing
and where raw emotion rules over all
Simple thoughts are drowned in despair

Mundane fears create pounding, surging seas
Welcome to Fantasy Island
where you can only be consumed
by dreams and wishes
Where you live in a system of self-mutilation and false praise

Welcome to the Conditional Sea
where ships upon it toss you out
if not for
your conversion to the Captain's religion.
Welcome to my world
where nothing is forgiven
where repentance does nothing to banish the memory.
Welcome to the world of trivial pursuits
where anything high budget succeeds
Welcome to the land where mouse chases cat,
and vultures grow hair.
You have fallen here
and there is no escape.
This house of cards belongs to you
you built it for me after all
So now I enjoy watching you suffering
In the reality created by you, for me
I choose to walk away
because birds look strange without feathers.
Life looks strange without life

Passing By

Tomorrow never looks like today
Until it comes
Happiness never seems to want to stay
It always runs away
Time is cruel as it passes by
But it never tells a lie

Ancient fears follow me
Hauntingly
Nightmares keep me from being free
This is the way it will always be
Life is cruel as it passes by
And it never tells a lie

Juggling emotion
And everyday life
Praying everything will be all right
Can I keep going on?
Will my pain go away someday?
Will my silent tears stop falling?
Soul, please stop dying...

1998

...I hold fast to my imaginings...

Imaginings

I know you are above me,
In a better place
But I'm selfish and wish you were here,
And I'm sad because my wish never comes true.
So, I imagine your smile is the rainbow,

Your love,	the radiant sun
Your laughter,	the babbling brook
Your tears,	the gently falling rain.
Your secrets,	the drifting snow.

I hold fast to my imaginings,
And look forward to the day
You and I
Together
Will watch the rising of the sun
Once again.

Lullaby

Go to sleep little baby,
close your eyes.
Go to sleep precious angel,
Darling one.
As you dream may you see all
the ones who love you,
and hold your heart
until the end of time.

Call On Me

Today your life doesn't seem worth living,
Your heart is breaking for what seems the last time.
You don't have anyone to talk to,
And today your tears may fall like rain.

Tomorrow may be an awful day,
You may retreat for what seems the last time
Turn to me I'll be here to talk to
You can cry upon my shoulder

When you need someone to talk to,
Call on me.
When you need someone beside you,
Call on me.
I'll always be here,
And I'll always understand.
Don't be afraid to call on me.
Call on me.

Morning, Noon and Night,
I'll be here for you.
I'll help you through the strife,
All through, the rest of your life.
Just call on me.

No Return

Connection severed
Your thoughts
Disappear
You break the silver thread
Attached to our souls
Because I'm no use anymore

Emptiness consumes
This part
Essence
You yanked away
Taking your dreams
Worries, fears
To the point of no return.

Stilled voice,
whispers silenced
Knife
Struck once with deadly force
Cold, unfeeling metal
Stealing my twin away.

Regret's Demons

Regret came to me tonight
And when she left, she unleashed her demons
                        to torment me.
Some danced around me as they sang of the
                        Monster I would become.
Other sat and told horrific tales of what I'd done
                        in the past.
How long will this nightmare last?

Regret's demons keen all around
Surrounding me
Horrifying me
Finally, they are silenced -
She returned
But when I faced her
I saw myself.
My mind reeled as I realized that I am Regret
Her demons my past, my fears

They vanished
      as dawn stretched her fingers of light across the sky.

I go about my day and feel the weight
                of my sins on my shoulders
My back and neck ache
                with the strain of bearing my
burden.
I wait for the night with dread,
for the demon's dance will begin again.

Solitude

It's three in the morning,
and I'm restless despite my exhaustion.
My memories are haunting me
wispy ghosts from the past.

I finally fell asleep
but my dreams weren't dreams at all.
White figures chasing me,
my heart racing at every sound.

Seeing all the wrong I've done,
    in every nightmare that I have.
Hearing my screams in the night
    as I mourn my sorrows.
Someone please, bring a light
    to chase these ghosts into the shadows.

Guide me home...
Give me solitude

Someday

I spend all my days waiting for you,
hoping you'll happen to drop by.
I spend all my nights dreaming of you,
hoping you'll come the next day.
Everywhere I go, I'm searching for you
hoping that I'll catch your eyes
And though I may not see you today
I'll keep hope for tomorrow
I know our paths will cross again,
someday.

Coyote

I stand alone
In this barren wasteland called "my life"
There are no hills or valleys
Just dust and gullies
With a scattered cactus or two

I am the prey
Of a coyote in the night
The once hunter being hunted in my nightmares
My body screams for sleep
My mouth cries for water
But I don't care enough to provide the nourishment I need
I just stumble along

I cry for rain
Oh, that this desert would succumb to the downpour
But there's so much pride and confusion
And no obvious resolution
so the clouds refuse to come.

My body's growing weaker
My eyes searching for a place to rest
My heart's mourning for love
My soul crying for an end to this torment
Please let peace and love rain down on me
Quench this dying soul

Understand me
Listen to my reason
Love me for who I am
Not what you think I should be
Your love and acceptance
Would take me form this desert.

Ghost

Wrapped within my
Shawl of mourning
Here
In this room of strangers
I should know

You
Walk right through me
Invade my sacred space
Without thought or feeling

I sit here on the floor
Punishing myself by
Staying in your presence

Lost
Within this darkness
Of me
I watch you forget that
I once was.

Deep
In this cave of entrapment
Searching for safe passage
To a place called home

I sit here on the ground
Punishing myself by
Believing your every lie

Possessed

Playing games
With letters
Sounds
Twisting, reforming
Creating a music-less song.
The curve of handwriting
Singing of love, death
Redemption.

Heart springs forth
Ready to play
Word games
Telling a story
In six lines
If the mood leads

I ache for the sight of
The music filled page
Heart owning the minstrel
Minstrel owning the pen
Using each other to
Make experience immortal.

Black Hole

I mold my hand
To the face of the
Man that you once were
Your eyes see beyond me
Into a world
Known only to you
You're blind to all
Except pain
You deny reality
Without shame

I memorize the shape
Of the beloved face before me
Too bad the fates
Are pulling you away
This goodbye
Is killing me slowly
You walk away
No indication
You ever cared

Wax mask
Painted by your colorful past
Anguished eyes
Impassive face
You've never been showered with grace

This love stands here
Unshrouded
But you're blinded
By the heat of the sun.

Destiny's Call

Destiny is calling,
I hear her sweet voice.
She beckons me,
"Follow, I will lead you to happiness."
Can I give up the darkness of my past?
Yes.
Time is mending the wounds,
The memories are fading from my mind.
There is hope for me,
The desert hasn't a hold anymore
Regret has faded away.
I stand complete
Ready to heed Destiny's call.

1997

...in this life there is a balance...

Nova

How come the ones so worth knowing
Are never known?
So like the snow slowly falling,
They melt away
When the sun returns.
They trickle through all
Just like the ones who were before them,
While we mourn one more star.

How come the ones who shine the brightest
Are the first to fall?
You always want what you can't hold onto
And sometimes what you've never known
They shone
Just like all the ones who were before them
And just as quickly gone.
While we mourn another stranger.

The Balance of Life

For Clorissa

As I look upon her sleeping face,
I see peace and so much grace.
But as I think about her future,
I see all she must endure.
The obstructions in her future,
The pain and anger too.

As I look upon her sleeping face,
I see peace and so much grace.
And as I think about her future,
I see all that she'll enjoy.
The excitement in her future,
The love and laughter too.

So, as I watch her sleep so peacefully,
In the future I hope she'll understand,
That in this life there is a balance
Of constant ups and downs.

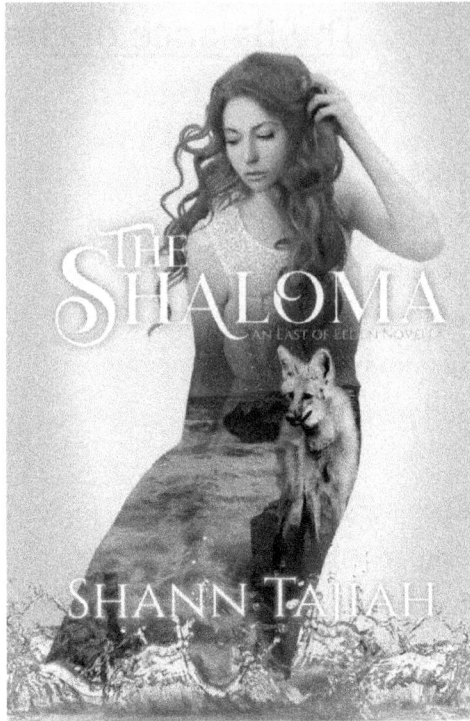

Now available in eBook and paperback!

Banished from society and branded a witch, Javicia is left to die at the hands of the elements or the savage beasts that guard the borders of Eeden.

The Foxkin have been guarding Eeden's secrets for generations, but the humans have become fearless and are willing to risk everything to discover what the beautiful forest hides.

Called by the Most High to stop the conflict, Javicia hides among the Foxkin, determined to leave humanity to its fate. But when the safety of those she loves is thrown into the balance, will she choose survival or sacrifice?

The Shaloma is the recipient of the 2021 CWC Writing Contest First in Fiction and Mary Carey awards.

SHANN TAJIAH is an
award-winning poet,
photographer, and author.
*Scraps of Love: Poetry from the
Darkest Night 1997-2010* is
her first poetry collection.

A Minnesota grown Texan,
Shann began her writing
journey when she was eight,
and by age thirteen she was
submitting for publication She
is currently hard at work on the second installment of the East of
Eeden duology. She is also one half of the spectacular writing duo,
T.L. Gabriel, where she writes about worlds beyond the stars.

Her passion for writing and authors has led her to establish her
publishing imprint, Ithirial Rising Press, and she is currently
studying to be a certified book and writing coach.

When Shann isn't lost in the world of words, she can be found
spending time with her husband, daydreaming in her hammock, or
caring for her furred menagerie.

You can keep up with her adventures at www.shanntajiah.com or
on YouTube and Instagram @authorshanntajiah

www.ingramcontent.com/pod-product-compliance
Lightning Source LLC
LaVergne TN
LVHW011152080426
835508LV00007B/361